Spiritual Grounding and Shielding

A SPIRITUAL WORKBOOK

Professor T. Matthew Brown

**Copyright © 2024 by T. Matthew Brown.
All rights reserved.**
No part of this publication may be reproduced, stored in a retrieval system, or transmitted in any form or by any means electronic, mechanical, photocopying, recording, scanning, or otherwise, without the author's prior written permission.

Limit of Liability/Disclaimer of Warranty:

This publication provides accurate and authoritative information regarding the subject matter covered. We sell it with the understanding that neither the author nor the publisher are engaged in rendering legal, investment, accounting, or other professional services. While the publisher and author have used their best efforts in preparing this book, they make no representations or warranties concerning the accuracy or completeness of the book's contents and expressly disclaim any implied warranties of merchantability or fitness for a particular purpose.

Sales representatives may create or extend no warranty or written sales materials. The advice and strategies contained within may not be suitable for your situation. You should consult with a professional when appropriate. Neither the publisher nor the author shall be liable for any loss of profit or any other commercial damages, including but not limited to special, incidental, consequential, personal, or other damages.

GROUNDING AND
SHIELDING WORKBOOK
By T. MATTHEW BROWN
Cover design and illustrations
by Leitreanna Brown
Edited and formatted by
VAPBooks,
VAPBooks Publishing,
Virginia, USA.

TABLE OF CONTENTS

Introduction 8

Understanding Grounding 11

Why Grounding is Essential? 14

The Science of Grounding 20

Symptoms of Being Ungrounded 22

How to Ground Yourself: Expanded Techniques 24

Daily Grounding Practice: Making Grounding a Habit 30

Lifelong Benefits of Grounding..........................33

How to Ground Yourself: Practical Techniques 35

Understanding Shielding.38

How to Shield Yourself: Practical Techniques 41

The Interplay Between Grounding and Shielding 44

Conclusion 47

About the Author..............49

Introduction

Welcome to this session on *Spiritual Grounding and Shielding*, two fundamental practices that anchor us physically and spiritually. In today's increasingly fast-paced world, the demands on our energy are immense. We encounter emotional turbulence, stress, and even negative influences that can affect our well-being. Grounding and shielding, though often overlooked, are essential tools that help us maintain balance, restore inner peace, and protect our energy fields from unwanted disturbances.

Maintaining your spiritual, emotional, and physical balance is essential in a world that often feels overwhelming, filled with both visible and invisible energies. Grounding and shielding are two foundational practices that empower us to navigate life with clarity, protection, and stability. These techniques form a bridge between our inner selves and the external world, helping us stay centered in the present moment and protect ourselves from the negative or disruptive energies we encounter.

Understanding Grounding

Grounding is the practice of connecting your body, mind, and spirit to the stabilizing energy of the Earth. Much like the roots of a tree that draw strength and nourishment from the soil, grounding allows us to anchor ourselves, giving us a solid foundation to navigate life's challenges.

At its core, grounding is the practice of aligning your energy with the Earth's natural frequencies. It's a process of connecting your physical, emotional, mental, and spiritual bodies to the stabilizing energy of the planet. Grounding draws its significance from the idea that, like any electrical system, our bodies can accumulate excess energy—whether it's emotional stress, mental clutter, or external influences. We release this excess energy by grounding and becoming balanced, calm, and fully present.

In spiritual and holistic practices, grounding is a

powerful tool for reconnecting with the Earth, allowing us to feel rooted and supported. When we are grounded, external factors do not sway us, but operate from a place of inner strength and clarity.

Why Grounding is Essential?

Stability and Presence in the Physical World

In today's world, distractions—social media, work demands, personal relationships — and more constantly bombarding us. This often pulls us away from the present moment. Grounding helps us reconnect to the here and now. When grounded, we are fully present in our bodies and aware of our surroundings, allowing us to better focus on tasks, engage with people authentically, and make clear decisions.

Release of Excess Energy and Emotions

Many of us carry emotional burdens or pent-up energy throughout the day. Without grounding, this excess energy can build up, leading to feelings of anxiety, stress, overwhelm, or even physical symptoms like headaches or fatigue. Grounding offers a release, allowing us to offload what no longer serves us into the Earth, where it can be neutralized. Just as lightning grounds itself to the Earth during a storm, we too can ground our emotional storms and find calm.

Restores Balance to the Mind, Body, and Spirit

When we are disconnected from the Earth's energy, we often feel scattered, drained, or out of sync. Grounding restores balance between the physical and spiritual realms. It harmonizes the flow of energy through our bodies, promoting overall well-being and allowing us to function optimally. This balance is critical for mental clarity, emotional stability, and physical health.

Enhanced Spiritual Awareness and Connection

Grounding is a key spiritual practice that enhances our connection to higher realms. Many people mistakenly think that grounding is only about connecting to the physical world, but it also opens us to spiritual awareness. By being firmly rooted in the Earth, we create a solid foundation from which we can explore higher dimensions of consciousness. Grounding allows us to receive intuitive insights, spiritual guidance, and creative inspiration without being overwhelmed by them.

A Tool for Energetic Protection

Grounding not only centers us, but it also strengthens our energetic boundaries. When we are ungrounded, we are more susceptible to external influences and negative energies. Grounding acts as a protective mechanism, creating a sense of stability and inner strength that prevents us from being easily affected by the energy of others or the environment. When we are firmly grounded, we are less likely to be drained by energy vampires or emotionally tumultuous situations.

The Science of Grounding

Grounding also has roots in science, particularly in the field of "earthing." This practice suggests that direct physical contact with the Earth (such as walking barefoot) allows the body to absorb electrons from the ground, which act as antioxidants. These electrons can neutralize free radicals in the body, reducing inflammation, improving sleep, and even enhancing cardiovascular health.

Research has shown that grounding can have tangible benefits for the body's physiological processes. For instance, it can lower stress hormone levels (cortisol), reduce muscle tension, and promote faster injury recovery. The Earth's electrical charge can help rebalance the body's bioelectrical fields, improving physical health.

Symptoms of Being Ungrounded

Being ungrounded can manifest itself in various ways. Some common signs include:

- Feeling spaced out, disconnected, or disoriented.

- Difficulty focusing or concentrating.

- Frequent anxiety, nervousness, or irritability.

- Feeling overwhelmed by the emotions or energies of others.

- Frequent exhaustion or lack of motivation.

- Overthinking and mental fog.

These symptoms reflect a disconnection between your physical body and the stabilizing energies of the Earth. Grounding is an essential practice to mitigate these effects and bring your energy back into harmony.

How to Ground Yourself: Expanded Techniques

Physical Connection with Nature

Nature offers one of the most effective ways to ground yourself. Walking barefoot on the Earth—whether grass, sand, or soil—allows your body to absorb the Earth's natural electrons, balancing your energy. Spending time in nature, gardening, or simply sitting under a tree can also help you reconnect to the Earth's stabilizing energy.

Visualization Practices

Grounding doesn't always require physical contact with the Earth. You can ground yourself through visualization, a powerful technique for realigning your energy. Imagine strong roots growing from your feet into the Earth's core. Visualize these roots expanding more profoundly and deeper into the ground, anchoring you firmly. As you breathe in, feel the Earth's nurturing energy flowing upward through these roots, replenishing and balancing your entire body. Any negative or excess energy is released into the Earth with each exhale.

Grounding with Breathwork

Controlled breathing is a simple yet effective grounding practice. Deep, slow breaths help calm the nervous system and draw your focus inward. Begin by taking a deep breath in for a count of four, holding for four, and then exhaling slowly for another count of four. With each exhale, imagine any tension or scattered thoughts leaving your body and dissipating into the ground beneath you.

Using Grounding Crystals

Crystals like hematite, black tourmaline, or red jasper are known for their grounding properties. Holding or wearing these stones can help anchor your energy and provide stability. You can meditate with them, carry them in your pocket, or place them around your home to encourage groundedness throughout the day.

Mindful Eating and Hydration

Grounding can also come from nurturing your physical body. Eating whole, nutritious foods and drinking plenty of water helps connect you to the Earth's resources. Root vegetables (carrots, potatoes, beets) have strong grounding properties, as they grow directly in the Earth. You reconnect to the physical world nourishingly when you eat mindfully, savoring each bite.

Exercise and Movement

Physical activity, especially forms that emphasize balance and body awareness, can help ground you. Practices like yoga, tai chi, or even simply walking with intention allow you to reconnect with your body and the Earth. Movement helps to release stagnant energy and brings your awareness back into the present moment.

Daily Grounding Practice: Making Grounding a Habit

For grounding to be most effective, it should be incorporated into your daily routine. Regular grounding helps maintain your energy balance and prevents the buildup of stress and negativity. Here's a simple grounding routine you can try:

1. **Morning Grounding:** Begin each day with a few minutes of barefoot contact

with the Earth (if possible) or a grounding meditation. Set your intention for the day, visualizing yourself being deeply rooted and centered.

2. **Midday Check-in:** At lunchtime, take a moment to breathe deeply and reconnect with the Earth. Eat mindfully and be fully present as you recharge your body.

3. **Evening Grounding:** Before bed, perform a grounding exercise to release any accumulated stress or energy from the day. This helps clear your mind and

body for a peaceful night's sleep.

Lifelong Benefits of Grounding

Grounding is not just a spiritual practice—it's a life-enhancing practice that reconnects us to the source of all life: the Earth. By grounding regularly, you cultivate a sense of stability, resilience, and inner peace, allowing you to navigate life's challenges with clarity and strength. As you ground yourself in the Earth's energy, you'll find that your body, mind, and spirit come into greater harmony, enabling you to live a more balanced and centered life.

When you are grounded, you are present, aware, and in harmony with your surroundings. Grounding helps you:

- **Center your energy:** Reducing feelings of anxiety, worry, or overwhelm.

- **Restore balance:** Bring stability to your physical, mental, and emotional bodies.

How to Ground Yourself: Practical Techniques

Earthing: One of the simplest ways to ground yourself is through physical contact with the Earth. Walking barefoot on grass, soil, or sand allows your body to absorb the Earth's natural energy directly.

Meditative Grounding: Imagine roots growing from the soles of your feet, extending deep into the Earth's core. Visualize the

Earth's nourishing energy flowing upward through these roots, revitalizing your entire being.

Breathwork: Slow, deliberate breathing is an excellent grounding tool. Focus on your breath and draw in stabilizing energy with each inhale. With each exhale, release any tension or negativity that does not belong to you.

Mindful Presence: Grounding is also about being fully present in the moment. Engage all five senses in your immediate environment. Feel

the texture of the ground,
listen to the ambient sounds,
and observe the world around
you with heightened
awareness.

Understanding Shielding

While grounding strengthens our connection to the Earth, shielding fortifies our connection to ourselves. Shielding creates a protective barrier around your energy field, safeguarding you from external negative influences, psychic attacks, and draining energies.

Imagine your aura as a bubble of energy surrounding your body. Just as a physical shield protects a knight in battle, spiritual shielding keeps harmful energies at bay while preserving your own energy.

Shielding is essential because it:

- **Protects your energy:** You may encounter people or environments that drain you emotionally or spiritually. Shielding helps maintain your energy integrity.

- **Prevents energetic leakage:** Your energy can dissipate without shielding, leaving you feeling fatigued or scattered.

- **Promotes a healthy energy exchange:** Shielding doesn't mean isolation. Instead, it allows for balanced, intentional interactions with others without the risk of being overwhelmed by their energy.

How to Shield Yourself: Practical Techniques

Visualize a Protective Shield: Close your eyes and envision a radiant bubble of light surrounding your entire body. The light can be any color that feels right to you—gold for divine protection, white for purity, or blue for calming energies. Picture this shield as impenetrable to negativity, yet porous to positive and loving energies.

Mantras and Affirmations: Simple phrases like, "I am safe and protected," or "Only positive energy surrounds me," repeated with conviction, can help fortify your energetic shield.

Crystals for Protection: Crystals such as black tourmaline, obsidian, or amethyst can act as powerful shielding tools. Carry them with you or place them in your home to create a protective energy barrier.

Cleansing and Reinforcement: Shielding

requires regular upkeep. Just as a physical shield can wear down, your spiritual shield needs periodic cleansing and reinforcement. Practices like smudging with sage or using salt baths help to cleanse your aura and renew your shield's strength.

The Interplay Between Grounding and Shielding

Grounding and shielding are complementary practices. Grounding is your inner strength, your rootedness in the Earth, while shielding is the outer armor that protects your personal space.

Here's an analogy: A well-grounded tree has deep roots and stands firm against the wind, but when a storm approaches, it's also wise to build a barrier around it for added protection. Similarly, we must ground ourselves in the Earth's energy while erecting spiritual boundaries to weather the storms of life.

To integrate both practices:

- Start with **grounding** to root yourself in stability.

- Then, visualize **shielding** to protect your aura from intrusive energies.

- Practice **self-awareness:** Regularly check in with yourself to ensure your shield

is intact and your grounding
connection is strong.

Conclusion

Spiritual grounding and shielding are vital components of energetic self-care. In a world where we constantly interact with diverse energies, protecting our own while staying rooted in the present is essential. By regularly practicing grounding, we can remain centered and stable, and through shielding, we can protect our energy, allowing us to navigate life's challenges with grace and resilience.

May you carry the wisdom of these practices with you, finding peace in grounding and strength in shielding as you continue your spiritual journey.

Thank you.

About the Author

In the eerie realms where the veil between our world and the supernatural thins, T. Matthew Brown is a seasoned explorer, a 25-year veteran who strides fearlessly into the unknown. His journey began in the crucible of his youth, a time when he confronted malevolent forces that defied explanation.

At a mere fifteen years of age, Matthew found himself thrust into the forefront of a battle against a violently haunted home, where shadows whispered secrets and unseen hands grasped for the living. In a testament to his unwavering courage, he engaged in spiritual warfare to shield his mother and six siblings from the sinister specters that plagued their every moment.

Matthew's fearless encounters with the paranormal did not end there. His investigations have been documented on screen, from chilling episodes of "Paranormal Witness," where his harrowing survival story captivated audiences, to ventures with the LMN Network that delved into the darkest corners of haunted history.

Recently, Matthew has joined forces with esteemed paranormal investigators Brandon Alvis and Mustafa Gatalori in their upcoming TV series "Family Spirits," a chilling exploration into ancestral hauntings airing on Haunt TV. His collaborations extend beyond television, venturing into the realms of YouTube sensations like Aldo's World, Moe Sargi, and Adventures with Angelo, where his expertise illuminates the darkest corners of the internet.

Beyond his media appearances, Matthew is a prolific author, having co-authored four spine-chilling books alongside his wife, Leitreanna Brown. Together, they unravel the mysteries of the paranormal, offering insights garnered from decades of research and firsthand encounters.

In the academic sphere, Matthew and Leitreanna are esteemed educators. They share their wisdom as instructors of Parapsychology at Piedmont Technical College and Christ the King Catholic College. Their teachings bridge the gap between theory and practice, empowering a new generation of investigators to navigate the supernatural with knowledge and respect, leaving them feeling informed and enlightened.

Never one to rest on past achievements, Matthew is currently at the forefront of paranormal innovation. With a keen eye for technological advancement, he is designing cutting-edge equipment set to revolutionize the field. A tantalizing announcement looms on the horizon, promising groundbreaking developments that will forever alter the way we perceive the unseen.

For T. Matthew Brown, the paranormal is not just a realm of mystery—it's a calling, a lifelong quest to uncover the truths that elude conventional understanding. With each investigation, each new discovery, he pushes the boundaries of what we dare to believe is possible, proving that in the shadows of the unknown, courage and curiosity can illuminate even the darkest of mysteries.

Made in the USA
Columbia, SC
05 October 2024